tarot

tarot

YOUR DESTINY REVEALED IN THE SECRETS OF THE CARDS

staci mendoza and david bourne

special photography by john freeman

southwater

This edition is published by Southwater

Distributed in the UK by
The Manning Partnership
251-253 London Road East
Batheaston
Bath BA1 7RL
UK
tel. (0044) 01225 852 727
fax (0044) 01225 852 852

Distributed in New Zealand by
Five Mile Press NZ
PO Box 33-1071
Takapuna
Auckland 9
New Zealand
tel. (0064) 9 4444 144
fax (0064) 9 4444 518

Distributed in Australia by
Sandstone Publishing
Unit 1, 360 Norton Street
Leichhardt
New South Wales 2040
Australia
tel. (0061) 2 9560 7888
fax (0061) 2 9560 7488

Southwater is an imprint of
Anness Publishing Limited
© 2000 Anness Publishing Limited

1 3 5 7 9 10 8 6 4 2

Publisher: Joanna Lorenz
Senior editor: Doreen Palamartschuk
Copy editor: Raje Airey
Photography: John Freeman
Design: Tania Monckton
Illustrators: Sarah Young and Tania Monckton
Editorial reader: Kate Sillence
Indexer: Hilary Bird
Production controller: Yolande Denny

Contents

Introduction

For hundreds of years, the Tarot has been a source of mystery and fascination, intriguing us with its compelling and enigmatic pictures and symbols. No one really knows where the Tarot originated, or how or why it works. One thing seems certain though: if we can "tune in" with the images presented to us on the cards, then we can gain access to a deeper understanding of ourselves and the people and events involved in our lives.

The Tarot deck as we know it is composed of 78 cards, which divide into two clear parts: the 22 cards of the Major Arcana and the 56 cards of the Minor Arcana. The Minor Arcana is further sub-divided into four suits: Wands, Swords, Cups and Pentacles. The Minor Arcana closely parallels a normal pack of 52 playing cards with its suits of Clubs, Swords, Hearts and Diamonds. The Major Arcana reflects the major turning points in our lives: our commitments, triumphs and tragedies, whilst the cards of the Minor Arcana deal with the more day-to-day

aspects of life. Taken together, they constitute a guidebook to the incidents and issues that we have to handle in our lives, from the past, the present and looking to the future.

This book is designed to be a practical reference guide to help you become acquainted with this ancient system of divination. It gives concise key background information to the Tarot, followed by general definitions for each of the cards. Finally, it suggests different tarot spreads and ways in which you can put this advice into practice by giving actual Tarot readings for yourself, friends and family.

Although this book contains general guidelines about what the cards mean, the ultimate aim is for you to develop your intuitive skills using the Tarot and to arrive at your own conclusions. In the end, each reader and their interpretation is as unique as a set of fingerprints. The Tarot has the potential to be original and fresh and perhaps this is why it is as popular today as it was hundreds of years ago.

Using Tarot Today

Almost everyone who is fascinated by the Tarot is interested in it primarily as a tool for divination and for developing psychic ability. The word "divination" comes from the same root in Latin as "divine". In many ancient cultures, divination was often regarded as sacred, or pertaining to the gods.

at all about the Tarot, simply by looking at the images, having a response and then conveying what is seen, felt and understood. The visual impact of the Tarot deck creates images clearly in our minds, which trigger our intuition and memories. The more we work with these images, the more our intuition and memory is stimulated and gradually our psychic ability can increase.

Today we can use the Tarot for many purposes: to ask for advice about a best course of action, to gain insight into life's spiritual "lessons", as a tool for meditation and self-discovery, and also to develop our psychic ability and interpret what we see for others.

The principal difference between the Tarot and other divinatory tools, such as crystals, numerology or astrology, is that the Tarot is a pictorial system. The pictures and strong images give this system an impact which is real and immediate and it is possible for some people to give accurate readings without knowing anything

However, whether you intend to use the Tarot to learn more about yourself and your situation, to give readings for friends, family and others, or to develop your psychic ability, remember that the study and practice of Tarot is to be enjoyed. Any insights you gain are to be communicated in a humane and kindly fashion and you should be constructive in giving advice. All information you discuss with anyone should stay confidential.

The Origins of Tarot

Above: *Portrait of Maria Sforza painted by Bonifacio Bembo (1447-78). The original tarot deck is named after the Sforza family.*

lthough the Tarot is one of the best-known forms of divination, its precise origins remain shrouded in mystery. The cards have existed in the form that we now know them for 200 years. Various theories have been put forward by esoteric scholars about their exact origins, some suggesting the cards are from ancient Egypt, others that they see strong links with Hebrew mysticism. However, the first real evidence of the Tarot's existence dates back to Renaissance Italy.

In the mid-15th century, the Duchy of Milan was ruled over by the Visconti family – a name that has remained synonymous with the cards. The Viscontis commissioned Bonifacio Bembo to paint a set of 78 unnamed and unnumbered cards that depicted religious allegories, social conditions and ideas of the time. They were painted to celebrate a marriage between the Sforza and Visconti families and formed the deck for an Italian gambling game called "Tarocchi". It is uncertain whether the cards had any esoteric significance at the time or if they were devised only for game playing.

In the late 18th century we find the Tarot cards recorded as being used as a divinatory tool. Between 1773–82, the Frenchman Antoine Court de Gébelin published an eight-volume work called *Le Monde Primitif*. Here he speculated on the origins of the Tarot (which was the French name for Tarocchi), and offered the view that the cards originated in ancient Egypt and were in use there as a book of magical wisdom. At the time of de Gébelin, there was considerable interest in Egypt, and many people believed that Egyptian hieroglyphs were magical symbols concealing lost knowledge of the past. The ground was therefore fertile for de Gébelin's theory which gained credence with many people.

Following in the footsteps of de Gébelin came Tarot students, each one of whom added to the links and analogies that make the current Tarot. This development reached its height in the 19th and early 20th centuries. In 1854, the book *Transcendental Magic* was published in France. Its

Above: *Filippo Maria Visconti, 1392–1447, a member of the wealthy family that commissioned the first tarot deck.*

author was Alphonse Louis Constance, originally a deacon in the Catholic church, but better known by his Hebrew pen-name, Eliphas Lévi. He linked each of the 22 cards of the Major Arcana with one of the 22 letters from the Hebrew alphabet. Lévi was the first person to insist on a link between the Kabbalah, a Jewish mystic tradition with its own system of esoteric thought, and the Tarot, saying that one could not be understood without the other.

Right: *Portrait of Aleister Crowley (1875-1947) by Augustus John.*

It was Lévi's system, still in use by many French occultists today, that provided a stepping stone for one of the most well-known Western magical orders to begin their work: the secret Order of the Golden Dawn, founded *c.*1886. Its members took up the Tarot, and began developments that would lead to new schools of thought. These changes were largely brought about by the work of two of its members: Arthur Edward Waite and Aleister Crowley.

In 1909, Waite commissioned the American artist Pamela Coleman-Smith to paint a set of images for his "rectified" Tarot. This deck of cards, known as the Rider-Waite Tarot (Rider was the London company that published them)

became one of the most influential Tarot decks of the 20th century. It is used all over the world today. It was the first deck to depart from tradition by using pictures for the numbered suits of the Minor Arcana.

Crowley had a reputation as an actor, magician and a womanizer, but he was also a serious esoteric scholar and Kabbalist. In the early 20th century, he decided to create his own deck and asked Lady Frieda Harris to paint it. The Thoth Tarot was published in 1969, but neither Crowley nor Harris lived to see it.

Above: King of Woods *watercolour by Frieda Harris 1941, from the Tarot pack designed by Aleister Crowley.*

Crawley modernized the existing deck by re-positioning The Fool, the unnumbered Major Arcana card, at the start of his Tarot deck, and transposed the Justice and Strength cards. Crowley also included a system of astrological connections with each of the Major cards, thus departing from the traditional French system.

The Aspects of Tarot

The Tarot is designed to relate, pictorially, to what we are feeling inside. It reflects our psychological and emotional state as well as showing us the people and events involved in our lives. The aim is to use the images on the cards as a springboard, allowing their own intuitive meaning to come through. However, the following general guidelines may be applied.

The symbolism and meanings of the Tarot, as presented on the following pages, are taken from a popular and traditional point of view. They represent an overview of the basic imagery that has been present in many forms in the cards during their history.

Today there are hundreds of Tarot decks, each with their own vision and ideas about the Tarot. However, although a lot of decks will look very different to the descriptions in this book, in most cases these descriptions will remain valid.

When you buy a new pack, all the cards will come in numerical and sequential order. To learn each card's definition, it is probably useful to follow this order. Once the definitions have been mastered though, there is no need to keep the cards in any order.

When reading the cards for yourself or others, some people like to distinguish between Upright and Reversed directions.

UPRIGHT

This refers to the card when it is facing pictorially upright when it is laid out in a Tarot spread right-side up. It reflects the meaning of the card in its purest form.

REVERSED

This direction refers to the card when it is facing upside-down in a spread. The reversed direction can indicate a subtle change or significantly alter the meaning of the card.

Aces

The Ace is the crowning card in any deck. Mathematically valued as either one or eleven, it is usually a matter of personal choice as to which way you want it to add up. It can be used to win in card-playing games due to its mathematical duality. This theme of winning or victory is also present in the Tarot and Aces are usually seen as extremely positive cards and as the keystones of the Minor Arcana.

The Aces contain the powerful energy of the entire suit that they represent, the absolute truth of that particular element, whether it is fire, water, air or earth. They are of great help when approaching any new or difficult situation. The Ace cards are from the suits of Wands, Pentacles, Cups and Swords. The Major Arcana has no Ace card but the unnumbered Fool takes up its place in this grouping.

Eights

The Eights have a special role and are particularly important in a reading. This is because the figure eight (8) relates to the symbol of infinity, the never-ending cycle of life in which our lives spiral, always constant yet always changing. Any of the Eights will therefore highlight changes in our lives, the sense of moving forward. These cards are the eighth Major Arcana card, Strength or Justice (depending on the pack), and the Eights in the suits of Wands, Pentacles, Cups and Swords.

The Major Arcana

There are 21 numbered cards in the Major Arcana, plus the unnumbered Fool, totalling 22 cards altogether. The 21 cards reflect major turning points in life. They represent states which affect all of us at some time or position in our lives and which we all have to go through. As the Major Arcana cards are so significant, they will always take special precedence in a Tarot spread, reflecting the more important and challenging points in our lives.

The cards of the Major Arcana can be broken down into three segments, each consisting of seven cards. The first group of seven cards deals with the realm of the Material World, such as material comforts, the choices made which reflect and influence physical life, and higher education. The second group of seven deals with the realm of the Intuitive Mind.

This covers aspects such as faith searching, using our free will, love and its effect of change in our lives, and psychic understanding. The third group of seven is concerned with the combination of the first two groups and forms the realm of Changing Issues. This last group of seven contains the most significant and powerful cards in the entire deck as they have the added bonus of challenging or altering the path of life we are actually on.

In addition to these three groups of seven which divide the Major Arcana, astrology also plays a part in the Tarot deck. The Sun, the Moon, the twelve signs of the zodiac and the planets of our solar system, are all reflected within the cards of the Major Arcana, while the four suits of the Minor Arcana have astrological associations with the four classical elements of astrology: Earth, Air, Fire and Water.

0 The Fool

The only oddity of the Major Arcana is the Fool, whose number is zero. In medieval times, the Fool held a special place in society. For many people, he was an innocent in contact with the gods and was able to say and do more or less anything he liked. It is this idea that still held sway and influenced the card imagery of the Fool when the Tarot was developed, and thus the Fool jumped into the Major Arcana in its own unique and individual way.

The Fool does not fit into any of the three sections of seven in the Major Arcana and so it can be placed either at the beginning or at the end of the Major group, in a similar way to the Aces of the Minor Suits. This decision is traditionally left to the individual to decide for themselves, but for the purposes of this book and for learning the Major Arcana definitions, the Fool has been placed at the beginning.

Traditionally, the fool is represented as a young, androgynous figure with a look of wonder in his eyes. He is sniffing a beautiful rose so intently that he does not notice he is just about to step over a dangerous cliff. The figure carries a staff with a bag attached to it, whilst at his heels a white animal snaps, almost as if it is trying to force the character over the ledge. The fool is seen as an adventurous card and the feeling of change is often associated with the fool.

PLANET OF
URANUS

UPRIGHT

This card denotes a fresh, new beginning and spontaneity. New experiences and directions are occuring so accept the process of change. You will be taking a risk or an unknown step forwards without really knowing the outcome, but the joy and excitement is in the experience of change and not in the end result.

REVERSED

A foolish individual who does not think before they venture out, hence they frequently make considerable mistakes in life. It would be much better to stop and take time to evaluate matters and plans before forging ahead. This could also indicate a childish view of life and not accepting responsibilities.

The Realm of the Material World

The seven cards in the first group of the Major Arcana deal with situations that are connected to commitment through society's laws, such as marriage, success, higher education and the family.

I   The Magician

PLANET
OF
MERCURY

A man wearing long robes stands behind a table. His left hand is raised, pointing towards the sky. In it he holds a wand. His other hand is empty, but lowered, pointing towards the ground. Before him on the table lies a sword, a cup, a wand and a pentacle (or coin). Above his head there is an infinity symbol and surrounding him are flowers and other greenery.

UPRIGHT

This is a preparation card, warning you to bring all the elements of your life together: love, emotions, action, finances and morality. This is in preparation for changes ahead so that you can handle situations correctly.

REVERSED

An individual who conducts themselves with great presence and perfectionism and who appears to always have it "together". A person who handles chaotic situations and circumstances effortlessly and with ease.

II   The High Priestess

THE
MOON

A woman in long draping robes sits between two pillars. The pillar on the left is dark whilst the one on the right is light. Between them hangs a veil behind which can be seen a flowing stream. The woman holds a book with TARO written on it and wears the symbol of the crescent moon.

UPRIGHT

Trust your intuition. Don't take things at face value but look behind the scenes. Look for answers to your questions from within your heart. Use logic less to come to the right conclusion.

REVERSED

Everything is out in the open, nothing is hidden and all the facts are obvious. You are now able to make your decision with confidence, using both intuition and logic.

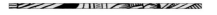

III   The Empress

The Empress is represented by a voluptuous woman – often with fair hair, clothed in a long flowing dress and smiling serenely. She wears a crown and in her left hand she holds a sceptre with a globe on the end of it. In her other hand she has a protective shield with the symbol of an eagle on it. She is normally depicted seated in natural surroundings and behind her a stream flows. For women, she represents security and motherhood.

PLANET OF VENUS

UPRIGHT	REVERSED
This is the key card to indicate fertility or pregnancy. If it comes up for a man or a woman outside child-bearing years, its meaning is one of domestic bliss, the feeling that "all is well in your home". The Empress represents a woman who has the ability to make people feel welcomed and loved in her own home.	An earthy woman whose main enjoyment in life is to care for others. A woman who by her own nature could not turn a soul away when they are in need. When reversed, the Empress can also mean disharmony in the home due to outside influences such as the visit of a difficult relative or a disruptive child.

IV   The Emperor

The Emperor is represented by an older man sitting on an unseen throne. In his right hand he holds a sceptre and in his left he holds an imperial orb with a cross on it, which is a sign of authority. Sometimes he has a large eagle on his hat. He signifies a male influence and confidence and worldly power and a person well capable of using authority.

SIGN OF ARIES

UPRIGHT	REVERSED
This deals with any form of established organization, such as banks, schools, governmental offices or established companies. It could also mean that you are trying to establish a company or organization of your own.	Disorganization and conflict with established organizations. Perhaps taking for granted an established reputation or position of authority, leading to complacency. It is now time to take action and point out where there are problems.

V The Hierophant

Also known as "The High Priest", this figure is the male counterpart of the High Priestess. Like her, he also sits between two pillars but his are both the same colour. He is dressed in the robes of a churchman and wears a triple papal crown.

He offers a benediction with his right hand and in his left hand he holds a sceptre with a cross on the top. Before him kneel two supplicants and at his feet are two keys. He represents professional advice, teaching and learning.

UPRIGHT	REVERSED
This card shows the need to seek professional advice from people such as doctors, lawyers and financial advisers. Alternatively, any ritualistic service that is performed under the eyes and jurisdiction of the Church, such as marriage, christenings, or divorce.	A person who lives their life according to society's rules, a follower, usually quite an academic person, such as an accountant, lawyer or doctor. Usually this will also represent a stable and successful individual.

VI The Lovers

A young man stands at a crossroads that branches off to the right and left. On each path a woman waits. The fair-haired woman stands on the right and the dark-haired on the left.

Above the man flies Cupid or an angel, offering him the choice of either of these two paths. This card usually indicates love or possibly the beginning of a romance.

SIGN OF
GEMINI

UPRIGHT	REVERSED
Instant chemistry between two people. An intimate relationship formed by a chance meeting, in which fate plays a part, such as missing your train by seconds, but taking the next one and meeting "Mr" or "Ms Right" on that train.	An individual who challenges society's rules regarding gender roles. This includes people who do not fall into a particular stereotype.

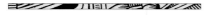

VII   The Chariot

A strong-looking figure rides in a chariot pulled by two sphinxes. In many decks the sphinx, or perhaps a horse, on the left is light and the one on the right is dark, meaning good and evil. In the man's right hand there is a wand or sceptre. The canopy of the chariot is covered in stars.

SIGN OF CANCER

UPRIGHT

A triumphant victory in life, which was quite a challenge to win. Even though you may be facing many obstacles, there is the feeling that what you are doing is the right thing.

REVERSED

At this time, it would be unwise to apply any more pressure to the situation concerned. If you do, you risk pushing people or circumstances over the limit and failing through applying too much pressure.

The Realm of the Intuitive Mind

The second group of seven Major Arcana cards focuses more on the individual than on society and worldly concerns. Decisions are based more on how you feel rather than on what you think. This section deals with circumstances that really touch our hearts.

VIII   Justice

A woman sits on a throne. In her left hand she holds a set of scales and in her other a great double-edged sword. She is often blindfolded. This card indicates fairness and balance. Sometimes this card can occur as number 11 in some decks and Strength as number 8.

SIGN OF LIBRA

UPRIGHT

Justice will now be served. This is a very favourable card in a karmic sense, because whatever the outcome of a particular circumstance, it will be a fair one.

REVERSED

An injustice will take place. The outcome of a particular circumstance will be unfair. It can also indicate bias and inbalance.

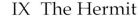

IX The Hermit

PLANET
OF
JUPITER

An old man stands at the top of a high mountain. He wears the dark robes of a monk and in one hand he holds a staff. In his other hand he holds a lantern which he shines before him. The light from the lantern emits rays of light that resemble the beams of a star.

UPRIGHT

You need to take time out just for yourself in order to regain your energies and gather your thoughts together once more. Take refuge in your own company and try to do the things that will make you happy. Be more self-aware.

REVERSED

An individual who finds it difficult to take the advice of others and hence at times suffers for their pride. It is good to consider the advice of other people at this time because they are well-meaning and have your best interests at heart.

X The Wheel of Fortune

SIGN OF
VIRGO

There is a wheel in the centre of the card with Fortune in the middle. In some decks the letters TARO are written upon the wheel in the position of the four cardinal points – north, south, east and west – as if the wheel were a compass. Sometimes figures or animals climb up the outside of the wheel. In this deck at the top of the wheel on a platform is a sphinx, in other decks it is often a man with ass's ears. The card indicates destiny and fate.

UPRIGHT

Fate will now take a strong hand in life and redirect the path that you are on. Sometimes this change can be really positive, such as an award for merit, or it can be something negative, such as a job redundancy. Either way the matter is beyond your control, but the path taken after this redirection is in your own hands. Stay adaptable and take advantage of chance events.

REVERSED

Although you may have been finding that life and your fortunes have been a little difficult of late and you may have experienced a run of bad luck, this card indicates that things are changing and your life will be soon taking a turn for the better. Everything is on the way up again and now it is time to herald and enjoy the positive changes that are coming in your direction.

XI Strength

SIGN OF LEO

The strength or fortitude card in most decks is represented by a young man or woman controlling a lion in some manner. The card indicates moral strength, self-discipline and courage. In some decks Strength is 8 and Justice is 11.

UPRIGHT	REVERSED
There is no need to worry, or lose sight of your goals. Even if the road you're on is difficult, you will get there in the end. Be patient and persevere. Have confidence in yourself.	You feel a need to seek reassurance from a trusted source in order to help you get back on track. It is time to re-evaluate your position and where you are going.

XII The Hanged Man

PLANET OF NEPTUNE

A young man hangs from a tree by his left leg. His right leg is folded behind the left, making a shape like the number four. His arms are folded behind his back. The man's face does not look tortured but quite serene.

UPRIGHT	REVERSED
Life is at a standstill or in a rut. Although things may not be to your liking, it is not as bad as you think. It is best to take life patiently at the moment and bide your time until you see that the timing is right to make the necessary changes and improvements to your situation.	A great contentment in life. You are feeling very happy with your present situation and the position in which you find yourself. Things are going so well at the moment that you feel you are almost blissful.

XIII Death

A skeletal figure wields a bow or large scythe. The ground is cracked and in some decks he is walking through a field of bones and cutting off the heads of figures that have been buried up to their necks in the earth. Generally this card means getting rid of the old to make way for the new.

SIGN OF SCORPIO

UPRIGHT	REVERSED
Regeneration and rebirth, the feeling that you have been given a new outlook on life and a fresh attitude on how to approach it. Sometimes this occurs when an unparalleled event takes place such as a near-death experience.	A refusal to let change happen, to let that which has run its course die. This can lead to a deep depression which may create the need to seek professional advice from a doctor, psychologist or experienced counsellor.

XIV Temperance

An angel-like figure holds two cups from which she pours liquid, one into the other. By the feet of the angel there is a pond of water. She has one foot placed in the pool and one foot placed on land. Temperance indicates moderation and blending of opposites.

SIGN OF SAGITTARIUS

UPRIGHT	REVERSED
You need to test the waters first, not dive in. Be patient and take things nice and slowly. "Go carefully where angels fear to tread." Exert some self-control.	This card indicates that it is now time to stop and re-evaluate the situation before you proceed with anything further in order to stop making the same mistakes over again.

The Realm of Changing Issues

The seven cards of the final group of the Major Arcana are the most revered of all the Major cards because they go beyond society and the individual. They represent those universal laws and concerns that have the power to bring about the kind of circumstances and events that can alter the course and path of our lives.

XV   The Devil

A large figure, half-man and half-beast in appearance, stands on a pedestal. He has horns and the wings of a bat or bird. Two figures with horns, a man and a woman or sometimes lesser devils, are chained by heavy rope to the pedestal below him by the neck.

SIGN OF
CAPRICORN

UPRIGHT

This indicates new-found passions, energy and enthusiasm. Rediscovering your innermost passions and having the energy and impetus to act on them.

REVERSED

Obsessions, addictions, and compulsive behaviour. When passion goes wrong or is directed in a negative manner, seeing a given situation with any clarity is almost impossible.

XVI   The Tower

A high tower is being struck by a lightning bolt. As a result of the explosion, fire leaps from the tower and figures fall to their doom at the base of the building.

PLANET
OF MARS

UPRIGHT

Complete and unforeseen disruptions and disagreements in life that are sudden or unplanned and are therefore difficult to deal with. Abandoning past ties.

REVERSED

The worst of the disruptions are now over and it is time to piece your life back together in a way that is more suitable and positive.

XVII   The Star

SIGN OF
AQUARIUS

Many stars shine above a woman in the night sky. In other decks a naked woman kneels beside a pool. She holds two cups from which she pours liquid onto the land and back into the pool.

UPRIGHT	REVERSED
A wish come true, usually something you have thought of since childhood, such as meeting the perfect partner, or the ideal career opportunity.	What once seemed like a dream come true is no longer so appealing. Now that you have your desire, you wonder if it was worth it.

XVIII   The Moon

SIGN OF
PISCES

Two dogs bay up at a large shining moon. In other decks a woman holds a crescent moon.

UPRIGHT	REVERSED
Take a close look behind the scenes as someone or something is not what it seems. There is a risk here that you are being lied to. Take another look at the situation and ask more questions.	Lies or deceptions are taking place. It would be best to become detached from a particular person or situation at this time because neither is likely to change.

XIX   The Sun

THE SUN

A yellow sun shines down on a verdant garden of flowers in which a child or young person plays.

UPRIGHT	REVERSED
An extremely positive card indicating growth and an increase of potential in all or many areas of life, such as progression in relationships, financial expansion, and physical growth (as in pregnancy).	Look at your life clearly, seeing it for what it actually is and not what you think it is. Re-evaluate your situation to make better progress and have a clearer sense of purpose and direction.

XX Judgement

Two angels fly above the earth blowing trumpets. Below, people rise from a tomb with their arms and hands held open towards the sky. In the Visconti-Sforza deck a godly figure appears at the top of the card. This card symbolizes an end of a situation and then rejuvenation and regeneration.

PLANET OF
PLUTO

UPRIGHT

An indication that what has been holding you up and kept you in a rut is ending – a change will occur. You are now free to move forwards with a more positive demeanour and attitude. The lifting of karmic restrictions.

REVERSED

Poor judgement. This could keep you at a standstill or in a rut if you are not careful about the choices you make at this point. Take time to evaluate the direction you really want to take before proceeding.

XXI The World

In some decks two children support a globe-like object. In other decks a hermaphroditic figure dances lightly as if on air. In both hands she holds white wands whilst around her there is a wreath with no join. From all four corners of the card the same four beasts that are present on the Wheel of Fortune look inwards towards the dancing figure.

PLANET OF
SATURN

UPRIGHT

This is by far the most auspicious card in the deck. It indicates great success for the individual in all areas of life. Total success and contentment are what is available to you now.

REVERSED

A fear of your own success in life. It is as though the goal is within reach, but you hesitate to take it – perhaps through fear of it not being quite deserved or fear of being disappointed.

The Minor Arcana

Although it is possible to do Tarot readings using only the Major Arcana cards, the story would not really be complete without the 56 cards of the Minor Arcana which correspond to the 56 cards of a modern deck of playing cards.

So far as we know, the Tarot was designed to be used as a total unit, comprising both the Major and Minor Arcana. The Major cards deal with life's grand gestures, showing us the main theme at a particular time. Its sister group, the Minor Arcana, completes the balance by showing us the finer and more ordinary details of our lives, such as the people, places, events and day-to-day circumstances.

The Minor Arcana is broken down into four separate suits of fourteen cards each, Cups, Wands, Pentacles and Swords, which correspond to Hearts, Clubs, Diamonds and Spades on a modern deck. Their numerical order runs from ace to ten (pip cards), with four court cards, Page, Knight, Queen and King, to finish the sequence. Some modern Tarot decks use Prince and Princess cards as the Page and Knight.

The four suits deal with different, yet equally significant, areas and aspects of life. The suit of Cups deals with our emotions and issues that occur with love and relationships. The suit of Wands deals with physical actions and activities and our ambitions. The suit of Pentacles deals with all aspects of security, such as our finances, careers, home and family. And finally, the suit of Swords deals with moral issues and the conflicts that can arise as a result.

Although the cards of the Major Arcana have a dramatic impact, daily life is more likely to be made up of lots of little areas and incidents, some of which can seem quite boring or insignificant. These are shown by the Minor Arcana. It is by combining these two distinct parts of the Tarot deck that you are given a more in-depth and realistic interpretation of life and its circumstances.

The Court Cards

The four Court Cards form part of the Minor Arcana and represent people or personality traits.

Although these cards stem from an old-fashioned and traditional view of male and female roles, the attributes discussed can be applied to anyone, regardless of age, gender, sexuality, race, or creed, unless specifically stated.

Pages

In former times, pages were young people who worked in the royal courts, bringing messages, notices and letters. They served at table, helped lords and ladies dress and did a multitude of other things. Being a page was the young person's education for a good position in life, hopefully leading to a knighthood. In the Tarot deck, the Pages are not specifically male or female. They can represent some or all of the following elements: children, messages, communication (such as telephone, letter, e-mail or another medium), information being given and passed on, studying, or apprenticeship.

Knights

In the days of chivalry, knights were young men who served the king and his court. They were sent out on errands, to find new lands, make new discoveries, forge new ties and test their skills. In the Tarot, the Knights are figures of action, they take up quests – whether the goal is self-discovery and finding your purpose in life, or challenging misfortune and injustice on behalf of others. In today's society, where both men and women share the workplace and life's responsibilities, it is important to remember that Knights can be male or female.

Queen

The queen was the mature partner of the king. Queens will primarily represent women, and traditional female concerns: the home, relationships and emotional nurturing. A Queen can also represent a man who exhibits qualities or concerns in these areas.

King

The king was the ruler of the land whose duty was to maintain law and order. Kings will primarily represent men and traditional male concerns: ruling, responsibility and decision-making. A King can represent a woman who exhibits qualities or concerns in these areas.

The Suit of Swords

When the Swords are present in a reading, the issues that are indicated by this suit concern any situations or actions to do with morality, moral conflict and conflicts in general. Think of an actual sword. It is sharply pointed, double-edged and made of strong metal, such as steel.

In the Arthurian legend, the young King Arthur is set a test: to pull the immovable sword, Excalibur, from the stone. Arthur, because of his fine character and upstanding moral convictions, is able to pull the sword free and with great ease. In doing so, he exhibited some of the qualities of the suit of Swords: notably, strength of character, determination and the ability to see an action through with an outstanding result.

The suit of Swords is related to the astrological element of Air. The three Air signs of the zodiac, Libra, Gemini and Aquarius, are reflected in the suit of Swords. Like their astrological counterparts, this gives the people portrayed on the cards of Swords an analytical intellect. The thought behind the action is the key importance of this suit. In some foreign-language Tarot packs, the suit of Swords is called *Epée*, *Schwerter* or *Espados*. Swords equate to the suit of Spades in a pack of playing cards.

Ace of Swords

Upright

Victory and triumph after some difficulties and lots of hard work. This time you have really achieved and it's been you alone who has done all the work. When the victory or triumph comes, it cannot be taken away because of all the hard work and struggle you have had to put in. Well-deserved success.

Reversed

You must not put any more pressure on to a person or situation as you are in danger of pushing things over the edge. It would be best to sit back and allow the person or situation to calm down for a while even though it may be frustrating for you.

Two of Swords

UPRIGHT

Imposed self-protection, a wall is being put up between you and the outside world. This is usually due to upsetting situations which have taken place in the past causing you to build up your defences to guard against the pain of the past, present or future.

REVERSED

You are being far too overprotective and not allowing anyone to get close to you. This is almost to the point of becoming a hermit. Be more open-minded.

Three of Swords

UPRIGHT

You may experience heartache through a love triangle: for example you, your husband and your lover; you, your mother and your sister; or you, your best friend and your girlfriend. Someone, if not all three people, will get hurt through choices that need to be made.

REVERSED

Indicates heartache through a love triangle as for the upright position but on a less serious scale. This may be due to disagreements, slight jealousies and insecurities, which can more easily be resolved.

Four of Swords

UPRIGHT

You need to take some time out to rest, recover and recuperate. This is in order to gather your energies for a difficult situation that lies ahead. This can also come up after a difficult situation, telling you there is a real need to rest now.

REVERSED

Now you have rested you are ready to take life and its challenges on again. You are able to enter the rat-race once more.

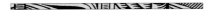

Five of Swords

UPRIGHT

A rift or argument has happened and you must deal with this. You have succeeded in proving an important point and your opinion has been heard and noted.

REVERSED

Now you have made your point, there is no need to be petulant and rub salt into the wounds or you could be accused of being ruthless.

Six of Swords

UPRIGHT

You are moving out of rough or anxious times and into smoother waters. Your situation or emotions will change. Life is on the up and problems will be dealt with more easily.

REVERSED

This card could indicate a delay or that your situation is improving, but not quite so smoothly or as quickly as you would like it to.

Seven of Swords

UPRIGHT

Through your pride or not knowing how to say "no", you are taking on more than you can handle and biting off more than you can chew. You need to be more diplomatic.

REVERSED

Certain pressures or problems that you have experienced in your life are now beginning to ease up.

Eight of Swords

UPRIGHT

There are restrictions on your ability to get on with your life freely. This could include, for example, living with a partner who is possessive, growing up with parents who have a severely strict outlook on life, or being restricted through disability, pregnancy, culture or faith.

REVERSED

The feelings of frustration or the restrictions that have been imposed on you are now being lifted, enabling you to move your life forwards and become more positive.

Nine of Swords

UPRIGHT

You are suffering from intense worries or stresses which may lead to sleepless nights. You feel overwhelmed by these anxieties.

REVERSED

The stresses or worries have intensified, leading to anxiety and fear. This is quite a serious problem at this stage and it is best to seek a professional opinion on such matters.

Ten of Swords

UPRIGHT

Your feelings have been deeply hurt from a situation or by a person that you were not expecting to be hurt by. This will be a painful experience but it will come to an end.

REVERSED

Great pain or heartache will be inflicted on you intentionally by a person or situation.

The Court Cards of Swords

Like a sharp sword made of steel, these characters tend to have a strong physical build with well-defined bone structure. Equally strong are their moral convictions and sense of right and wrong: these types will tend to look at life as black or white. They have a tendency to be serious and take their responsibilities in hand with great zeal and commitment.

Page of Swords

UPRIGHT
A wonderful feeling of enthusiasm, excitement and a desire to take life head-on will come over you. This is similar to the kind of feeling you may have on New Year's Day.

REVERSED
A person is behaving frantically and impulsively, usually from great excitement.

Knight of Swords

UPRIGHT
An individual with great determination to achieve their goals, but also a person of great loyalty and conviction and strength of character. He or she will diligently pursue their aims whilst respecting and caring for others.

REVERSED
An individual whose zealous conviction has led them to behave erratically and brashly, at times stepping on other people's feelings with their cold and indifferent behaviour. Take care not to act irrationally.

Queen of Swords

UPRIGHT

This woman is often a leader in her family or social group, carrying the moral load of keeping her friends and family together. She can be stubborn and not easily persuaded to change her mind or views on life but is also extremely loyal to her loved ones. Although she has few close friends, those lucky enough to have her loyalty will have it for life. In appearance she will like clean-cut designs and styles of fashion. Her general demeanour is of someone strong, solid and reliable yet possibly a little aloof or distant.

REVERSED

In outward appearance she is very similar to the upright Queen, but when reversed the Queen of Swords can become quite extreme in her personality, harshly judging others who do not conform to her critical eye. She can be unflinching in her stubbornness and at times could easily be accused of "cutting off her nose to spite her face". She can be very difficult to get close to emotionally and can come across as being cold and aloof.

King of Swords

UPRIGHT

A man who prefers the known and proven to the unknown. He will often have quite a fixed routine in his daily life, such as eating the same foods. The King of Swords has strong loyalties and would rather suffer then break them. He has a strong sense of responsibility and will not let people down when they rely on him for support. He is sensible yet also emotional, but does not wear his heart on his sleeve. Often conservative in appearance, he prefers clean-defined cuts, with practical, comfortable designs that are not showy.

REVERSED

A man who can be overly regimented and military in his routines. He is also rather harsh and cruel in his judgements of others or anything that does not fit into clear stereotypes. He could be accused of having a narrow outlook on life, without room for accepting new people, new ideas and new situations. Physically he is similar in appearance to the King of Swords upright. Intolerance and narrow-mindedness are the key factors of this card and you may come into contact with someone like this.

The Suit of Wands

When Wands are present in a reading, the issues that happen under this suit are connected with physical activity and action. Wands are concerned with the "here and now" – situations and plans that are being actioned in the present time. You can think of Wands as the "go, go, go" suit, because whenever these cards show up in a reading there is usually a lot of hubbub and activity surrounding them. Wands indicate a creative energy and can indicate an extrovert quality.

They are also associated with intuition. The suit of Wands is related to the element of Fire and it is this element that puts the action and imagination into the Wands. Aries, Leo and Sagittarius are the three fire signs of the zodiac that are connected to this suit.

Other names for this suit are Rods, Staves, Sceptres, Sticks or Batons. In some foreign-language Tarot packs, Wands are called *Bastoni*, *Stabe* or *Bastos*. They equate to the playing card suit of Clubs.

Ace of Wands

UPRIGHT	REVERSED
Put quite simply, the time to act on an idea is now! If you are planning any ventures or special tasks, now is the right time to get them in the pipeline and get things moving. Karmically speaking, this moment in time is most auspicious for the future of any given project or issue.	Plans or projects are currently put on hold or there is a lack of interest. Although it may be frustrating to wait, it is not the right time to proceed at the moment and it is more advantageous to wait until the timing intuitively feels better.

Two of Wands

UPRIGHT

Now is a good time to bring new people into your life and to share what you have to offer through friendship and lifestyle. Expanding our circle of friends and contacts can increase our happiness, because life can be quite meaningless without someone else or others to share it with.

REVERSED

Someone who is living the solitary life of a hermit and not finding happiness in that lifestyle. Now is the time to take drastic measures to become more socially involved, perhaps by taking up activities that involve a varied group of people. The alternative is to face the reality of living life alone.

Three of Wands

UPRIGHT

It is time to pursue new interests or directions in life. A new path is opening up and if you go down it, it will bring positive and good things into your life. This could indicate, for example, taking up higher learning, a particular hobby, or beginning to research a subject that interests you.

REVERSED

You are being too passive, waiting for life to happen to you and any new directions to become absolutely obvious before you make a move. It is time to formulate new directions and ideas about the path that you can follow. Decide what it is you are interested in, or good at, and take action.

Four of Wands

UPRIGHT

There is a warm and festive feeling in your life at the moment. Now is a good time to emphasise your feeling of goodwill by getting friends and family together to share in these positive vibrations. This could be through an informal get-together, such as a weekend away, a barbecue, a picnic, or a party.

REVERSED

You feel fed up with the general feeling of inertia and boredom in your life. You need to move yourself out of the rut by taking physical action, such as changing your scenery by taking a holiday, or redecorating your surroundings or doing something completely new.

Five of Wands

UPRIGHT

Discussions and mild debates are taking place at the moment so as to clear the air on certain subjects or issues. Usually these discussions are beneficial and can lead to greater harmony and understanding between the parties involved.

REVERSED

This card indicates that there is a degree of discord and disharmony in current discussions or negotiations. Consequently, the matter that is under discussion will require time and patience before it is resolved.

Six of Wands

UPRIGHT

You will receive public recognition and admiration from a job that is well done. Your peer group and those closest to you give you good support for your actions. You feel satisfied with your efforts.

REVERSED

This card indicates that you will finally receive the recognition due to you from a good deed or achievement from the past. You will be given thanks for your previous efforts and a task well done.

Seven of Wands

UPRIGHT

You will need to protect and defend your current position in life. It's time to watch out for the competition in a personal or professional capacity, but provided you keep on guard and have your wits about you, you should have no problems.

REVERSED

This card shows that your defences are down and you have feelings of self-doubt. You are in danger of being caught off-guard by someone or something in either a personal or professional capacity.

Eight of Wands

UPRIGHT

Life is moving in the fast lane. Look and see which cards fall next to this card in a reading, as their course of action will be speeded up. For example, the Lovers next to the Eight would be a relationship happening quickly, or the World next to the Eight would mean success is imminent.

REVERSED

For some reason, things have slowed down in your life and are grinding to a halt or you may feel misdirected. You will need to re-evaluate your current position in case you are unsure or confused before pushing ahead with new ideas and directions.

Nine of Wands

UPRIGHT

There is a chance that you are being overly defensive or suspicious and in danger of becoming paranoid about a current person, event or situation. It is best to examine your feelings quite carefully before you over-react dramatically.

REVERSED

Your suspicions have been verified and it is time to move on in your life. The best advice is to look to the future and not to get too engrossed or involved in the problems of the past.

Ten of Wands

UPRIGHT

You are currently going through a lot of stresses and strains. You have many responsibilities but you are quite capable of handling them so don't worry too much.

REVERSED

The stresses and strains of recent times have now subsided and you are beginning to feeling more contented. You can now relax and start to take things easy.

The Court Cards of Wands

Wands are batons made from wood. Wands are associated with people who are at ease with communication: they have quick and clear speech and are often interested in higher learning or cultural interests. They are also "people's people". As Wands is the Fire suit and Fire is active and always on the move, so the Wands are also physically active, and may have a wiry or athletic physique. They can be exotic to look at, with interesting attractive faces. They

tend to have a healthy complexion with a nice flush of colour. Their hair may have reddish or golden tones to it, with a natural curl or wave.

Page of Wands

Upright	Reversed
The Page indicates news coming to you by post, telephone, or e-mail for example. It is information that will be of special interest and significance to you.	Precisely the same as the definition for an upright position, except that the news or information you receive will be coming from someone who is younger than yourself.

Knight of Wands

Upright	Reversed
A person who is soul searching. Someone who is looking for answers as to why they are here on earth. Until this person finds the answers they are looking for, it would be futile to try and pin them down in a committed relationship. Wait and you will be rewarded with a life-long friend or partner.	A person chaotically looking for answers to their life's existence. They never settle in one place or with one person long enough to really understand anything about life's meaning. Such chaos can lead to outbursts of temper from someone who is possibly too extreme in their passions.

Queen of Wands

UPRIGHT

A woman who has a deep desire to be the centre of attention. She is charismatic and charming and knows precisely how to use her charms in order to better herself in life. She is often exotic in appearance and prefers bright and striking colours or styles of fashion. She is crafty with her hands as well as her mind. She would do well to go into a public-oriented career where she would be able to occupy centre stage, such as sales, or the theatre.

REVERSED

Although similar to the upright Queen in many ways, when reversed she becomes utterly competitive and manipulative in order to be the centre of attention. More often than not she will put value on what she can win for herself and not on people. She is not the best person for keeping deep dark secrets – she may let the cat out of the bag in order to score popularity points with her peer group.

King of Wands

UPRIGHT

A man who is relaxed and non-judgemental, dealing with problems and people in his life with ease. He has a welcoming and giving nature that is devoid of any competitive streak. He prefers to be close to nature and needs to be in touch with it in order to feel grounded in life. He would make an excellent partner or friend to anyone who could appreciate his relaxed, understated philosophy. In appearance, he is as relaxed as his personality. Typical features include wavy hair with golden tints in it and a healthy build.

REVERSED

In many ways, the card indicates a man who is very similar to the upright King, except that when reversed he is rather eccentric. He could be a bit of an inventor who could lock himself away from humanity for long periods of time while he creates. He is not converse with "people skills" and owing to his highly ingenious mind he does not understand humanity and its blatant vulgarity at times and can appear intolerant or narrow-minded.

The Suit of Pentacles

When the Pentacles are present in a reading, the issues that fall under this suit are to do with security and the material elements of life. This is echoed by the shape of the pentacle itself which is a gold disk that symbolizes money.

The aspects of life covered by Pentacles concern such things as career, investments, family, marriage, children, home, and any of those things in life which give us security or a sense of belonging.

The suit of Pentacles is related to the element of Earth and the issues that come up with this suit concern our senses and things that ground and stabilize us. The three Earth signs of the zodiac connected with this suit are Taurus, Virgo and Capricorn.

The Pentacles can also be referred to as Disks, Coins, Money or Circles. In some foreign-language packs, they are called *Deniers*, *Denari*, *Munzen* or *Oros*. They equate to the playing card suit of Diamonds.

Ace of Pentacles

Upright

Great financial rewards or success concerning a security issue. This could be a sudden windfall or inheritance, or the feeling of finally achieving success in your chosen career. This is also the perfect card to indicate total success in a relationship, suggesting security and contentment.

Reversed

This card indicates a reversal of fortune that involves your financial situation or perhaps a relationship. This is a time of feeling "at your lowest point" and of experiencing the inner emptiness that can arise when there is no real security in your life.

Two of Pentacles

UPRIGHT

You need to keep your balancing act up for a bit longer. Don't make any decision to drop any one aspect of your life just yet: you will need more information before making that choice.

REVERSED

You are in a situation that is difficult to balance and you are in danger of losing control. Assessing then organizing your priorities would help considerably at this time.

Three of Pentacles

UPRIGHT

Signature on contracts or important paperwork. This could be a marriage certificate, an employment contract, mortgage or loan documents, or divorce papers, for example.

REVERSED

There will be a delay in signing contracts or official documents at this time. You could feel very frustrated.

Four of Pentacles

UPRIGHT

You have some real fears about finances and feel the need to hold on tight to your money. Perhaps you have had times in your life where you have experienced difficult financial stresses and worries. This has left you with an underlying insecurity towards finances and financial matters in general.

REVERSED

You may feel deeply insecure in financial matters. Although this may stem from a real cause in the past, it has left you fearful of spending money even when you are financially secure. You should pay attention to emotional matters and not lose sight of the really important aspects.

Five of Pentacles

UPRIGHT

This card warns of a financial disaster or loss of security of some kind that has occurred recently or else is on the way, such as a job loss, bankruptcy, divorce, losing your home, or general money losses of some kind.

REVERSED

The financial or security loss has already taken place and you may feel a sense of helplessness. The task of putting things back together should be taken in hand and progressed.

Six of Pentacles

UPRIGHT

You will be looked after or treated fairly regarding a security issue. An indication of generosity in a financial transaction, settlement or award, such as a large pay rise, a profitable house sale, a generous divorce or court settlement, for example.

REVERSED

You may receive unfair treatment around a security issue – not receiving a well-deserved pay rise, an unfair divorce or court settlement, or a poor return on a house sale. You are not happy about the outcome.

Seven of Pentacles

UPRIGHT

Now is a good time to spoil yourself or make an investment and get the benefits of your hard work. You may have some anxieties about money but this would not have any adverse effect on your finances at this time.

REVERSED

It is time to stop "saving up for a rainy day". This attitude towards your finances is no longer appropriate: now it is time to do something special for yourself.

Eight of Pentacles

Upright

You have a talent with your hands that could earn you financial rewards and, if developed and you become skilled, could even become a career. This card refers to any person who works with their hands, such as an artist, photographer, healer, craftsperson or writer.

Reversed

The talent is there in your hands, but it still needs some fine tuning. You may need to go on to higher learning or to practise your skill more often, so that you become proficient enough to proceed with a proper career in the given field of interest.

Nine of Pentacles

Upright

A woman who has a natural demeanour to attract a good lifestyle to herself. She looks competent and well cared for. If she has a partner, he is most likely to be successful.

Reversed

This card indicates a woman who at times can be ruthless in obtaining a good lifestyle for herself. She may marry or have an affair with a man purely for his money.

Ten of Pentacles

Upright

An established secure home, family or relationship. This can also indicate the actual building of a home, which is usually an older property in pleasant surroundings, where several generations of the family will enjoy its homely atmosphere.

Reversed

This card indicates disharmony or an interference in a usually secure, established home, such as petty quarrels, family feuds and potential disorganization. There could also be instability regarding the family and finances.

The Court Cards of Pentacles

The symbol of the golden pentacle or coin signifies money and security and the material side of life. The people represented by Pentacles are generally concerned, therefore, with matters of security. They tend to be very family oriented and are focused on all the trappings of a secure life, such as a good job with a strong career path, a stable home environment, having more than enough food in the cupboards, money in the bank and so on.

In appearance they tend to have a solid build, eyes that are deep-set and, more often then not, their hair colour is any shade of brown.

Page of Pentacles

Upright

News or information about security is coming your way. This may be a win of money, a birthday gift or a small inheritance. It may be that you hear of a job vacancy, and you get the job, or you have news about a pay rise.

Reversed

This card indicates that a person younger than yourself is giving you news or information in relation to security.

Knight of Pentacles

Upright

This person is determined to get ahead with their ambitions in life. They plan strategically, knowing exactly how to climb the ladder of success and will proceed to take the necessary steps to achieve their goal. This is a focused person.

Reversed

Similar to the upright Knight, but with the added element of ruthlessness. Moreover, these types will tend to burn their bridges as they continue to move up in the world, thereby making plenty of enemies along the way.

Queen of Pentacles

UPRIGHT

This card indicates a woman with strong maternal and material instincts. Whether or not she has children, she will make friends and family welcome in her home. Her domestic life is important to her and marriage and children are the path she often chooses. She will work hard to make her surroundings comfortable.

REVERSED

This woman goes ruthlessly towards a career or her goals, letting nothing or no one stand in her way. Often this is a reflection of a very insecure or unstable childhood. She overcompensates for security and love by chasing and obtaining financial success.

King of Pentacles

UPRIGHT

A successful and powerful man with a great sense of responsibility towards his family, friends and career. Often he is successful because he has had someone else to provide for, such as his family or his relationship. This has been the driving force which has motivated him towards success. He measures his achievements through the security of his family and he views himself through the continuity of the important relationships in his life; he does not come across as overconfident. Usually he will make a sympathetic and caring partner for a woman.

REVERSED

Primarily much the same as the upright card, but with one major exception: reversed this King has a massive chip on his shoulder and is very insecure about his role as a man in life. This may be due either to a failed marriage and his children not being particularly interested in him as a person, or to a failed business career. He finds it hard to let go of the past and this could make forming new and satisfying relationships difficult. This card can indicate weakness.

The Suit of Cups

When the suit of Cups is present in a reading, the issues are connected with love, our emotions and intuitive faculties. The symbol of the cup resembles a chalice or sacred drinking vessel and brings to mind the "Holy Grail", or the cup of life itself. Consequently the issues of the Cups cards have a spiritual quality to them, affecting our emotional and intuitive selves: they are about self-acceptance and self-love as well as love for another.

The suit of Cups is represented by the element of Water and like water, our emotions are influenced by the Moon. The Moon is powerful and mysterious, able to influence the tides of the planet. Just as the Moon waxes and wanes, so our moods constantly shift and change and our emotional lives are in a constant state of flux like the waters of the ocean. The three Water signs of the zodiac that are reflected in the suit of Cups are Cancer, Scorpio and Pisces.

Other names for the suit of Cups are Chalices or Goblets. In some Tarot packs they may be called *Coupes*, *Coppe*, *Kelche* or *Copas*. They equate to the playing card suit of Hearts.

Ace of Cups

UPRIGHT	REVERSED
This card is also known as "The Holy Grail" or "Cup of Life". Some readers consider it to be by far the most important card in the whole of the Tarot deck. It indicates a miracle of life, a blessing of some kind. This may be finding a soulmate, or conceiving a baby. Any situation or subject that the Ace of Cups is near will be blessed with great luck and good fortune.	This card denotes disappointment or sadness, or a person who is suffering from "The God Complex", believing that the world revolves around them. With such a huge ego this person tends to fall quite hard. They will need to come back down to earth and accept other people's views and feelings.

Two of Cups

UPRIGHT

The forming of an important relationship. The relationship is one built on common interests, friendship and a higher understanding of adult love and companionship. Usually it will span the march of time and grow and develop with you.

REVERSED

An argument or disagreement has taken place between two parties that is really quite petty. One or other party in the relationship needs to break the ice and make the important first move towards reconciliation.

Three of Cups

UPRIGHT

This card denotes rejoicing, optimism and growth. It is a good time to enjoy yourself and indicates formal celebrations of events such as weddings, anniversaries, christenings, or a promotion.

REVERSED

Formal celebrations will meet with some discord. This may arise through personality conflicts, or bad timing in communications, such as things being said that would have been better dealt with at a different time and place.

Four of Cups

UPRIGHT

An offer of an emotional nature will be put to you, but it will come with strings attached. It would be wise to find out what these strings are first before accepting the offer.

REVERSED

You may be the victim of feeling that "the grass is greener on the other side" and have now got yourself emotionally involved in a situation that is not as good as it first seemed.

Five of Cups

UPRIGHT

You are in a situation in which an emotional sacrifice will need to be made, such as deciding between your husband and children and your lover. In this case the lover would be sacrificed because of the commitment to your family. Or perhaps a new friend is causing disruptions between you and your long-standing best friend. In this situation, the new friend will be sacrificed.

REVERSED

A similar type of sacrifice would have to be made as in the upright card, but in this instance it is less heart-rending. For example you may have to choose between your hobby or interest and your full-time career. In this case your full-time career is currently needing more of your time and commitment, hence it might be the hobby or interest that will have to be sacrificed.

Six of Cups

UPRIGHT

This card shows that you are currently dealing with memories, such as those connected with a person from the past, childhood issues or even with children themselves.

REVERSED

Similar to the upright meaning except that in this case it indicates the recent past. You will be dealing with someone or a memory from the recent past, roughly within the last five years.

Seven of Cups

UPRIGHT

This card indicates that there are plenty of appealing opportunities on offer to you currently. Indeed, there are so many of them that you may be unsure of which one to choose. Whichever one you take up, however, will prove very rewarding and emotionally fulfilling.

REVERSED

Emotionally you are feeling in a bit of a rut and there seems to be no one interesting or nothing that fascinates you at the moment. Do not worry, this barren emotional time will quickly pass and there will be new experiences just around the corner.

Eight of Cups

UPRIGHT

All that has been familiar to you emotionally has now gone past its "sell-by date". For example, you realise that the relationship you have been secure in for the past five years is not for you anymore. So you decide to leave it, along with all of its comforts. This is about venturing out into the world alone, but being quite relieved to do so.

REVERSED

When this card occurs it indicates that you are on the path of finding yourself now and you are able to re-evaluate the past and previous situations and relationships more clearly. This enables you to abandon old habits or friendships that are not working and to move forwards to the future more positively.

Nine of Cups

UPRIGHT

You are feeling a sense of emotional abundance, sensuality and fulfilment, that "all is right with the world". This feeling is quite similar to the emotional bliss that some women experience when they are pregnant.

REVERSED

This card denotes complacency. Emotionally you are quite spoilt and maybe taking for granted the love you receive from others. There may also be the feeling that you are never satisfied with your life.

Ten of Cups

UPRIGHT

A fresh, new start in the home. This can be an actual new home, or introducing a new aspect to the existing one – such as a child, a new partner, or even making structural changes to the property, which will make it feel completely different, fresh and new.

REVERSED

You will experience stress on the domestic front due to a disruption or a new introduction into the home. These stresses, although hard work, will usually work themselves through given some time and patience.

The Court Cards of Cups

The legendary cup of the Holy Grail is alleged to contain the waters of eternal life, one sip being enough to replenish, nourish and fulfil us all as humans. The people of Cups can be nourishing in a similar way, with their kind and loving natures. They are deeply emotional people and usually spiritual. They need love in their lives to feel alive and may put love before life itself. Their gentle natures do not know the meaning of the word "no" and they find it hard to hurt the people they care about.

Physically these types are sensual and usually attractive to look at. With soft skin and no sharp-angled bones protruding, they give the appearance of softness and fleshiness. Often their hair is fine and billowy, and they have large gentle eyes that gaze at another with great empathy. The colours they prefer to wear will be

delicate and sensual, such as purples, blues, silvers, creams and most shades of burgundies and pinks. They will choose their clothes by texture, liking such fabrics as plush velvets, silks and linens, for example. They prefer jewellery that is unique in its setting and have a liking for antique or specially designed pieces.

Page of Cups

UPRIGHT

This card is always present in a reading when a person is trying to gain your affection or attention. Often it is common for it to come up when you are dating a new person, or when it is your birthday or when someone close is trying to make up after a disagreement. This card is informally known as "The Courtship Card".

REVERSED

The reversed card is very similar to the upright definition of the Page of Cups, except that the attention will come from a person younger than yourself.

Knight of Cups

UPRIGHT

When the Knight of Cups is present in a reading you are being wooed and it can indicate a lover. It concerns matters of the heart, whether this is an actual love affair or other things such as artistic self-expression. Perhaps a new partner is putting on their best behaviour to court you.

REVERSED

This card denotes a person will be flirtatious, wanting affection due to their own insecurities and lack of self-worth. More often than not love is a sport for them, in which they are adept at convincing you that they're worth falling in love with. This person tends to be lax with the truth.

Queen of Cups

UPRIGHT

This woman has an ability to listen to others and to be interested in what they have to say. She is captivating and naturally charming and has a sensual, understated look that attracts others to her. The Queen of Cups makes a wonderful partner, friend, mother and colleague.

REVERSED

Similar to the upright Queen, except now she is plagued by deeply-rooted insecurity, doubting herself and her appearance. This means that she may stay in relationships and friendships where her good nature is taken advantage of and she is taken for granted.

King of Cups

UPRIGHT

This man enjoys socializing, entertaining and people in general. He is at his best when he has an audience that appreciates him. He is creative and is drawn to the world of art, theatre and music. He has great presence, a vibrant personality, and wears bright colours and showy styles.

REVERSED

Like the reversed Queen, this man suffers from deep insecurities and has a tendency to get involved with people who are not good for him or to form destructive relationships. Owing to his need to be noticed, he will go to great lengths to get attention. He needs to watch out for depression.

A Quick Guide to the Minor Arcana

This numerical guide can be used as a quick reference to the Minor Arcana definitions by taking the general background definition to a particular suit and cross-referencing it with the generic numerical meaning for any card.

As an example, take the Nine of Cups. The definition to the suit of Cups concerns emotional and intuitive issues, whilst a general definition for any of the number nine cards concerns poise and contentment. By combining these two pieces of information, you can work out a general definition to the Nine of Cups which signifies emotional contentment in your or the querent's current life.

KING
Competition, realization.

QUEEN
Fulfilment, deep level of satisfaction, skill, maturity.

KNIGHT
Focus, single-mindedness.

PAGE
Information.

TEN
Hesitation, some resistance to change.

NINE
Integration, contentment.

EIGHT
Organization, evaluation, experience, commitments.

SEVEN
Imagination, options, variety of choice.

SIX
Poise, contentment, relaxation, victory.

FOUR
Manifestion, creation of a plan, ability to "hang on in there".

THREE
Clarification, plans made public, appreciation.

TWO
Affirmation, some sort of choice, pledge, commitment.

ACE
Potential, new beginnings.

FIVE
Adjustment, challenge, possible conflict.

Reading the Tarot

Almost as much energy needs to be put in before interpreting the Tarot cards as into the actual reading itself. It is important to create a calm environment, preferably with soft lighting, as the setting for a reading. Too much background noise or bright lights can disturb your concentration. Privacy is also vitally important because quite personal and adult subjects may be discussed while doing a reading for another person (the "querent"). Eye contact and a caring smile always help the querent to feel at ease when you are reading their cards.

The querent should concentrate on the subject or issue of their reading. At the same time, they should handle the cards, shuffling them in some way. As soon as the querent feels they have concentrated and handled the cards for long enough, they can stop. This process will be different for each individual. Some people will take only a short time to get their issues clear in their minds, whilst others will take longer to focus. However, it must be left up to the querent to decide when they are ready. They should pass you the deck when they finish.

It is during the shuffling process that some of the cards become reversed. This is caused by the querent either deliberately turning the cards around, or by dropping a few in the handling process and putting them back in the deck reversed. Either way it is the individual's unique handling of the cards that will determine how they fall when they are passed over to you to be interpreted.

When you finish a reading always ask the querent if they understand and accept the information you have given them. It is with this final step that you will be able to monitor your skill as a reader and learn how to read the cards effectively. For instance, perhaps everything that you said was true – then great! That will give you a real boost of confidence. Or maybe some was incorrect – the person will let you know either way. Even if the whole reading was incorrect, do not worry because remember you are still learning and we all learn through our mistakes.

1 CLEAR YOUR MIND – Try to let go of your own personal problems or issues. This will get easier with time, although if you have difficulty doing this now, try focusing your mind on one thing such as a rainbow or a sunrise.

3 SHUFFLE THE CARDS – It is vital to do this as it gives the cards a fresh start. The Tarot cards are larger than normal playing cards and this may take practice. Make sure you focus on keeping your mind clear whilst doing this.

2 CLEAR THE CARDS – Make sure all the cards are in the upright position before giving them to the querent. If he or she, through their handling of the deck, reverses certain cards that is their own choice. To give the querent someone else's reversed cards is unfair as their reading would then be influenced by the choices and vibrations of the previous person who handled the cards.

4 THE QUERENT PICKS THE MAIN ISSUE – Ask the querent to concentrate as clearly as possible on the issues or areas of life that they are currently concerned about. These will be the ones you will be interpreting for them.

5 THE QUERENT SHUFFLES THE PACK – Hand the querent the Tarot deck and ask them to shuffle the cards. They should be concentrating on the issues or areas they want to look into. When they feel that they have shuffled the cards for long enough, they should hand the complete deck back to you. It is important that the querent hands the deck back to you when they feel ready: remember that you are interpreting for another person and their issues.

7 READ THE CARDS – Remember that you are starting to learn and understand the Tarot. Until you become confident and experienced in reading it, you are practising to use it in future readings. Let the querent know that you are a beginner. If what you are interpreting does not make sense or is too delicate a subject to take up with the querent, it is best to use discretion and plead ignorance in order to take the pressure off.

6 LAY OUT A SPREAD – Using whichever spread you are the most comfortable with, draw your cards from the top of the deck. Lay them down in the correct sequence, face up. Learn more sequences and probably vary these.

8 DRAWING TO A CONCLUSION – When you have ascertained and interpreted all you can from the cards let the querent know you have finished. Ask if they have understood and accepted the information you have given them.

The Celtic Cross Spread

The Celtic Cross is the best Tarot spread to use when you have a specific question on your mind, such as "I have just had a job interview – will I get the job?" This spread is best used when you are looking for an answer to a question that can be clearly answered with a "yes" or "no". This is because it deals with one issue at a time. Lay the cards out following the order of the sequence shown. The position of each card refers to a different issue as listed below:

POSITION

1	PERSON IN QUESTION
2	POSSIBILITIES OR PROBLEMS
3	BEST COURSE OF ACTION
4	INFLUENCES FROM THE PAST
5	CURRENT ATMOSPHERE
6	SHORT-TERM FUTURE
7	THE PRESENT STATE OF THE SITUATION
8	OUTSIDE INFLUENCES
9	HOME ENVIRONMENT
10	THE QUERENT'S SUBCONSCIOUS FEELINGS
11	LONG-TERM FUTURE

The Celtic Cross Explained

1 PERSON IN QUESTION – The card in this position indicates the querent.

2 POSSIBILITIES OR PROBLEMS – This will either indicate possibilities for a solution and a positive way forwards, or problems that may occur along the way.

3 BEST COURSE OF ACTION – This shows the best course of action or the road to follow in order to achieve the desired outcome.

4 INFLUENCES FROM THE PAST – This card is about a person or something from the querent's past that is present now or affecting the current situation.

5 CURRENT ATMOSPHERE – This represents the mood of the situation. This may be light and positive or heavy and serious.

6 SHORT-TERM FUTURE – This represents how the situation will develop over the next three months.

7 THE PRESENT STATE OF THE SITUATION – This tells us whether or not the current situation is precarious or stable. It indicates where it is now in relation to the future outcome.

8 OUTSIDE INFLUENCES – This represents other people or issues that may have an effect on the desired outcome or that need to be taken into consideration.

9 HOME ENVIRONMENT – This tells us something about the querent's home environment at the present time.

10 THE QUERENT'S SUBCONSCIOUS FEELINGS – This indicates whether the querent feels positive or negative about the situation and its outcome.

11 THE LONG-TERM FUTURE – The final card of the spread represents the likely long-term outcome of the situation, forecasting over the next six to twelve months.

A Sample Reading of the Celtic Cross

THIS IS AN EXAMPLE OF A READING USING THE CELTIC CROSS SPREAD
FOR A FEMALE QUERENT.

DEATH

PERSON IN QUESTION
Meaning: This woman has a whole new outlook on her life, and has discovered new energy both mentally and physically.

BEST COURSE OF ACTION
Meaning: Advice and assistance will come from a very charming and caring man. His response to the issue may well be intuitive as he will be on familiar terms with her.

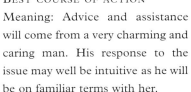

KING
OF CUPS

FIVE OF
SWORDS

POSSIBILITIES OR PROBLEMS
Meaning: She may feel the need to prove herself morally in the right, or to show that she is correct to have her new energetic feelings.

PAST INFLUENCE
Meaning: The situation she is dealing with is one she has been unable to resolve for some time. It is an old and current problem.

TWO OF
PENTACLES

CURRENT ATMOSPHERE
Meaning: Now she should take "time out" for herself to gather together all her thoughts and feelings and make the decisions that will be right for her.

THE
HERMIT

EIGHT OF CUPS

SHORT-TERM FUTURE

Meaning: Over the course of the next three months, this woman will be making an emotional departure from her old lifestyle and going in a new direction.

HOME ENVIRONMENT

Meaning: The woman is looking at her present home as a past-tense situation. A new home is likely in the near future.

SIX OF CUPS

PAGE OF CUPS

THE PRESENT STATE OF THE SITUATION

Meaning: She will be very popular and sought after as she moves in her new direction.

THE QUERENT'S SUBCONSCIOUS FEELINGS

Meaning: Subconsciously she feels in a bit of a rut and is looking forward to making even bigger changes when the time is right.

THE HANGED MAN

FOUR OF SWORDS

OUTSIDE INFLUENCES

Meaning: It would be best to keep her thoughts or opinions about her future direction, right or wrong, to herself. This is so that she can maintain some sort of control of her thoughts about her new direction.

LONG-TERM FUTURE

Meaning: The woman is right to trust her instincts and gut feelings about life. It is by following her intuition that she has been able to make the choices that she is now acting upon.

THE HIGH PRIESTESS

The Romany Spread

In the past, this spread was most used widely used by travelling fortune-tellers. It is also known as the Gypsy spread. Today many Tarot readers find it useful because it can look at a person's past, present and future together, thus giving them a more in-depth and overall picture.

The Romany spread is an effective spread to use when you want to find out what is generally going on in the querent's life, rather than looking for a definite answer to a particular question as in the Celtic Cross spread. It is best used when the querent has various issues that they are dealing with and they want to see how these things will pan out in the future. The querent is simply seeking some general insights into their current situation.

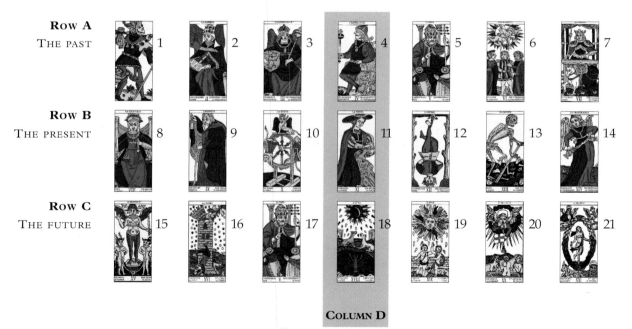

ROW A
THE PAST — 1 2 3 4 5 6 7

ROW B
THE PRESENT — 8 9 10 11 12 13 14

ROW C
THE FUTURE — 15 16 17 18 19 20 21

COLUMN D
PINPOINTING THE PERSON

The Romany Spread Explained

THE ROMANY SPREAD CONSISTS OF THREE ROWS OF SEVEN CARDS, CORRESPONDING TO THE PAST, PRESENT AND FUTURE. THE MIDDLE CARD OF EACH ROW FORMS A SEPARATE VERTICAL COLUMN, AND RELATES TO THE QUERENT. BEGIN READING WITH COLUMN D, THEN READ THE ROWS A, B, C FROM LEFT TO RIGHT.

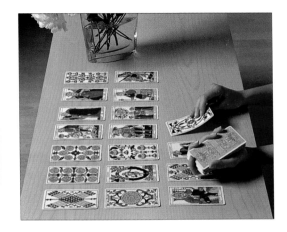

ROW A THE PAST
The first set of seven cards deals with the querent's past. Cards 1, 2 and 3 represent the more distant past whilst cards 5, 6 and 7 represent the more recent past.

ROW B THE PRESENT
The second set of seven cards engages with present-time issues that are going on for the querent. "What is going on right now!"

ROW C THE FUTURE
The final set of seven cards looks to the future of a person's life and what is likely to take place in this time. The future is taken to mean the span of time over the next eight months.

COLUMN D PINPOINTING THE PERSON
Cards 4, 11 and 18 form a central vertical column. By interpreting this small group of three cards, the reader can gain an insight as to what the querent is really curious or concerned about.

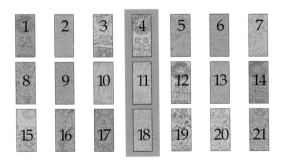

A Sample Romany or Gypsy Reading for a Male

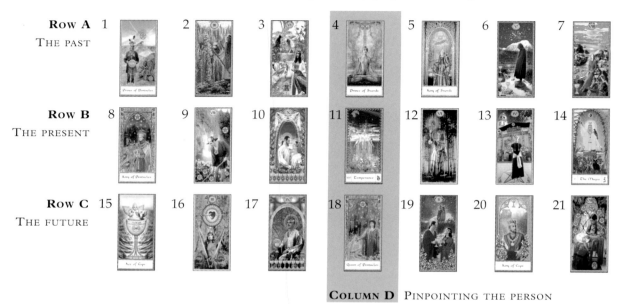

ROW A
THE PAST

1 2 3 4 5 6 7

ROW B
THE PRESENT

8 9 10 11 12 13 14

ROW C
THE FUTURE

15 16 17 18 19 20 21

COLUMN D PINPOINTING THE PERSON

COLUMN D – By looking first at column D (cards in positions 4, 11 and 18) you can deduce that this man is feeling emotionally balanced with a positive and focused attitude. There is also a nurturing and caring woman in his life.

ROW A – In the past, some information about a financial issue (possibly his career) led this man in a new direction, moving away from his childhood and past associations. This direction, which gave him a great feeling of excitement, turned into his way of life. Now he needs to put his trust and confidence in a new direction.

ROW B – As the querent has balance in his home life, he can take on new routines and improve his present situation. This can be best accomplished by being careful with finances and staying well organized.

ROW C – A blessing in disguise will take place for this man, but it means that a three-way emotional involvement will not work out. He should focus on the friendship of the strong, nurturing female in his life and make the association a firm partnership. By doing so, he will be able to achieve his creative endeavours.

A Sample Romany or Gypsy Reading for a Female

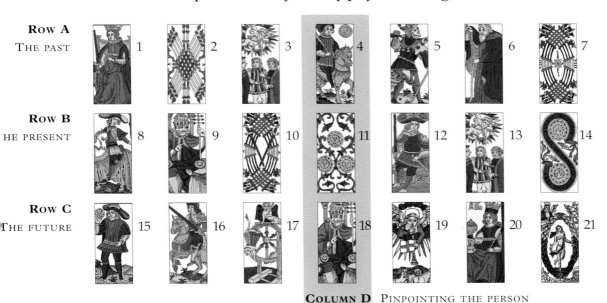

ROW A
THE PAST

ROW B
HE PRESENT

ROW C
THE FUTURE

COLUMN D PINPOINTING THE PERSON

COLUMN D – By looking first at column D (cards in positions 4, 11 and 18), you can deduce that this woman has some specific goals relating to her career. She is looking for more money and opportunities to support her interests.

ROW A – This woman has high moral standards and was stressed in the past due to her sense of fair play. Recently, she has embarked on a particular professional goal by taking new steps and a calculated risk at her own expense, leaving her feeling a bit isolated, like The Hermit.

ROW B – She is seeking professional advice about her situation, as she feels betrayed professionally by someone, or something has jeopardized her plans. She seems to have the support of a relaxed and philosophical partner who encourages her to make positive choices.

ROW C – She will soon receive news about a professional goal which will turn fate around in a positive direction, leaving her feeling more emotionally balanced. The final outcome is one of total success in all areas of her life.

A Final Word

Hopefully this book has touched on and answered some of your questions about the Tarot and also increased your interest to go on and learn more about this fascinating subject.

The Tarot is a user-friendly form of divination because of the highly visual prompts that each of the 78 cards contains. The mystery surrounding these almost timeless images stems from their enigmatic and historical past. For thousands of years, humans have practised the art of communication through the use of creative thought and storytelling. The Tarot is one of our greatest tools for continuing that art. By interpreting the Tarot's definitions with discretion and kindness for our friends and family, we continue this age-old practice of learning from the spoken word and picture.

The Tarot can be developed further as a tool by taking one card at a time and meditating on its visual imagery and then noticing the

thoughts and feelings that this imagery evokes. You can then cross-reference your discoveries with the card definition and see how they tally. In this way, you can build upon the historical and allegorical symbolism of the card, stamping it with your individual and contemporary experience. You can do this as many times with as many decks of cards as you like. It is a good idea to familiarize yourself with the imagery and symbols of more than one tarot deck. A useful thing to do while you are working through the deck like this is to keep a notebook. This will help fix the cards in your memory and provide you with a good source of reference material to look back on while you are working with the other cards.

Another process that further develops our understanding and learning of the Tarot is to explore its links with astrology. The connections between astrology and Tarot are interwoven, and although it may take some time to discover and understand them, it is well worth it. The best time for studying and practising the Tarot is when you have some peace and quiet. The cards are generally the size of a normal playing card and can easily be laid out more or less anywhere where you have a flat surface and where you feel comfortable. This could be sitting on the floor in your lounge, relaxing in natural surroundings, or even in your office. The most important thing is to make sure that you and the querent are relaxed and will not be disturbed.

Remember that the Tarot does not control fate or tell us how to live our lives. It can discuss the options and goings-on at a given time, giving us a clearer picture of where we stand, but ultimately our destiny lies in our own hands. The Tarot is there to be enjoyed for its lively communication, its honesty and its vision. It has the ability to heal through the pure and simple fact that someone cares enough to listen and advise.

When giving or receiving a reading, the best way of looking at this beautiful deck of cards is that it is like going to a good friend for advice. So please enjoy what you have learned from this book, use it wisely and with discretion and, most importantly, have fun.

Index

Acknowledgements
The authors would like to thank their students in the study of the Tarot: past, present and future. Through working with them over the years, the authors have evolved their own interests and further learning on this fascinating subject.

The publisher would like to thank the following individuals and agencies for loaning items for photography and for reproducing images:
Diane Flint for the loan of the pewter chalice (0208 809 0059 for commissions); Way Out There and Back – new age outlet for tarot decks (01903 722666; Suzanna at Mysteries Ltd., 9-11 Monmouth Street, London WC2H 9DA (0107 240 3688). p.13r AKG Picture Library; p.8l, p.9l, p.10c The Bridgeman Art Library; p.8r, p.9r, p.19r ETArchive. J. L. Chaumet p. 63. Illustrations from the Native American, Gendron, Pierpont Morgan Visconti-Sforza Tarot decks reproduced by permission of U. S. Games Systems, Inc., Stamford, CT. Images from Tarot of Marseilles reproduced by permission of U. S. Games Systems, Inc/Carta Mundi. Copyright © 1996 U. S. Games Systems, Inc/Carta Mundi. Further reproduction prohibited. Illustrations from the IJJ Swiss Tarot Cards and Tarot of the Old Path reproduced by permission of AGM Müller, CH-8212 Neuhausen, Switzerland. © 1972 By AGM AGMüller, Switzerland.